Today's Thoughts

TODAY'S THOUGHTS

Positive Thoughts for a Stressful Existence

BECOMING A WINNER
BEGINS IN THE MIND

Robert D. Pickard Jr

XULON PRESS

Xulon Press
2301 Lucien Way #415
Maitland, FL 32751
407.339.4217
www.xulonpress.com

Paperback ISBN-13: 978-1-66286-651-7
Ebook ISBN-13: 978-1-66286-652-4

Dedication

To my mom **Darlene Pickard R.I.P**, my biggest cheerleader. I celebrate you and thank you for everything you have done for me my whole life. Continue to lead the dancers in heaven. I wish you could have seen what I have done and celebrate with me I hope I'm making you proud.

To my wife **Kenda Pickard,** the love of my life, thank you for supporting me in my endeavors. We just made 20 years together and I toast you to another 20 years as we continue to grow together in love. Through everything we continue to grow learn and most of all in love. I hope you know that everything I do, I do for us. I love you more than you could ever know.

To **Kennedy** and **Josh,** you two have been the best kids that a father could have. Kennedy, keep dreaming and dancing but most of all growing. I'm proud of you, you are a beautiful young lady and never stop being the loving person that you are. Josh, you have been the kindest most respectful son that a man could have, I'm proud of the man that you have become keep achieving and being kind but most of all dependable.

To my Siblings **Mika, Patrick Pickard and, Dad** I thank both of you for supporting me in everything that I do. Mika, when mom passed you became mom #2 and know that everything that you have done, each meal or words of support will never be taken for granted by me. Pat, I'm proud of you little brother through everything you stayed strong, and you keep growing daily and I know that you will keep on the path to success. Dad thanks all the hard work that you put in while we were growing up and support.

To **Uncle Claude R.I.P** and **Aunt Susie,** you were the model of what a marriage should look like. I thank you both for the support my whole life. And I love you both. Uncle Claude you were a titan of a person, and I will say one of my biggest role models and the roadmap that I followed to become a man. Aunt Susie, you were the silent rock of the family. The greatness that Uncle Claude achieved couldn't been done without you. The stability that you provided in the home made it easy. And that is something that now days is a lost art.

To **Uncle Chucky R.I.P** and **Aunt Delores**, you helped me at a time when I was struggling in life and your love and advice got me back on track and I love you both. Uncle Chuckie, you were just what a 16-year-old me needed during a time that I was struggling in life. Yor wisdom and kindness helped me and kept me from going down the wrong path at a time where is could have been lost. Auntie, we have always had a special relationship and the support and love that was given to me from you has meant more than I could ever say. I thank you for all the advice and support, our talks for me were priceless and I know that you were always there for me.

To **Uncle AL**, and **Aunt Carlette**, what can I say about you both except you have been there for us so many times over the years. Uncle Al, there are so many things that you have done for me and my sibling and Mom over the years and just know that it didn't go unnoticed you are a great example of what fatherhood and being a husband should be. Auntie, for all our conversations all the laughs and wisdom that you shared over the years, I feel saying thank you is not enough you all are a great part of my village.

To my friends, **Geno, Pep, Marc, J.D., Kole, Dexter, Richard, Kev,** and my Cousins: **Jonny, Claude, Stephen, Lisa, Simone, Nicole, Antony, Pammy , Jean and all of my family members.** To my friends I could write a book on each one of our friendships and all of you have been there in hard times as well as the good. And I thank God for all of you every day.

To my family, all of you have poured into me in ways that I cannot repay each one of you have given me support in different ways and they a were all equally important. I wish I had room to write about all of you individually. I am doing this as a representation of you and I hope I am making you all proud. Most of all I want to thank God for giving me the inspiration, drive and most of all discipline that allow me to not only start but finish the project. God, you have kept me during both good and bad times. And for this I honor you.

Foreword

I am a person that loves people. My journey is one of humble beginnings and humble living. In my youth I understood that common sense living was the one thing that could keep you living harmoniously with others. I do not consider myself a guru or a counselor. However, what I do see in myself is a person that has seen many things and lived through more. And continues to live with a desire to lend a hand showing someone another option that could bring about the desired result in their life.

Lighting the path for others is an important task, having the desire to show the way is a result of learning life's lessons and putting them in action.

I started out a military man in search of himself. I then followed my passion of music and I love and still love all forms. I have Co-penned a Billboard #1 and another top five the Billboard chart. I have two degrees in Information Technology and am currently pursuing a master's degree in Information Technology. During the pandemic I talked to people and have heard story after story of hardship and loss. My family has experienced loss as well. And this was the fuel that propelled me to write my first book. Positivity can be the one thing that keeps people from taking their own life or the life of others. I just wanted to lend a hand a be a shoulder to say hey it will get better.

1. **Today's Thought… Something to think about, I was reading an article in which a writer was describing a person he saw in the airport he describes her long blond hair, her halter top and shorts that had Juicy printed on them and the stilettos on her feet. Yes, this 8-year-old girl was the hottest thing in the airport he stated. 😒 Please let children be children. Unbelievable.**

- The over sexualization of Youth is something that needs to be dealt with. Pedophiles and predators are lurking everywhere so the last thing that is needed are children being dressed up like adults and paraded around like fresh bait on a fishing line. Freedoms in America are things are constantly having boundaries tested and debated where the lines should be drawn as far as the protections of our rights are concerned. As a believer of a minimalist government the protection of freedoms are just as important as clean water and breathing fresh air. The truth remains that just because you can do something doesn't mean that you should. So, in that spirit govern yourselves accordingly.

2. Today's Thought...Pray for these young Black men. Well, no matter how much you want to protect your kids from life you can't. My son had a run in with the police that gave him a real reality check. He thought that because he keeps on the straight and narrow that he would be viewed by the content of his character and not the color of his skin. Well, he got a taste of American racism/ police profiling. So parents take out time to prepare your kids for this ugly reality called life...#racismsucks#

- Every time you turn on the television there is another story of a Black man getting killed by the police while being unarmed or just involved in a "routine" traffic stop. As a 14-year military man I want the support of the police if there is a threat that needs to be dealt with especially as a property owner and more importantly a human being. And as a father I want to know that when my son or daughter goes out into the world that they will be extended the same understanding that the average

3

white citizens receive. Having College age or Adult Children whenever you hear the phone ring during the night hours really keeps me on edge hoping that the call that is coming in is not going to become the next tragic headline in America.

3. Today's Thought....If you have a friend that has something good to say to you about the good things that happen in your life, only when things are good in their life, then I'd recommend that you have another friend that you can count on during their the bad times ....#Realtalk#

-   There are certain people that are only able to see the good in things when, things are good in their life. I call those people," the as long as friends ". Just as long as I am in a good place will I be able to rejoice in your good news. But the minute they are going through life's trials as they will come, just some how they can no longer see the good in your situation due to their own condition. A true friend will never allow their moment of discomfort dictate the level of loyalty shown to you and yes that is a form loyalty. Loyalty allows you to be the same no matter the situation. And if a person shows that they haven't achieved this level of growth, don't judge them but just understand who they are and share good news with those that have earned your trust.

4. **Today's Thought…Are your feelings your own? Or you a good impersonation of what everyone wants you to be?"**

- This is one of life's unfortunate truths where people are pressured to live in boxes created by others. It could be your parents, friends and even society's point of view. Just because your parents were Doctors, Lawyers or the business type doesn't mean that is where your passion will live. And if no one has told you, that is okay, be unapologetically you. That is where your greatness will lie in your passion. Everyone who has ever found greatness in an area that wasn't on the beaten path was considered crazy, until the genius of their passion was realized. And truthfully being the first at something is a lonely place to be especially until it was understood. It's hard to walk alone in your own lane but, it's also one of the most fulfilling places to be once you understand the purpose of your existence so be fearless and most of all be who you are created to be.

5. Today's Thought...Be Direct, it keeps confusion from occurring. Don't hint, Say. Then you can be sure ,when you say whatever it is and, if it doesn't change or happen, then you will know that it was intentional and not because someone didn't get the hint...#Makeitplain#

- This subject is one that I could have written a whole book written about it and is probably one of the most important topics when it comes to relationships and communication between people. Whether in the workplace or in your personal life speaking directly to the problem is probably the best was to gain clarity in most situations. Most things can be resolved by talking directly about the problem and first finding out if the other person understands what is being communicated in the first place. Nothing is more frustrating than being in a disagreement about something that was never discussed prior. Assumptions will always lead to disagreements, so don't assume, say because once you have done this then it removes any doubt whether the other person understood what was being discussed and acted intentionally.

6. Today's thought... Protect your energy. If you have people that state that they are in your corner, yet you always notice that there is something questionable coming out of their mouth in reference to your success, know that is how they really feel. Remove them from your circle, protect your peace.

- Have you ever been around someone that was always making little jokes about the good things that are happening for you? Yet never seeming to have anything truly positive to say. Make sure that you take note you don't even have to say a word, just remove yourself from the situation. Everyone doesn't deserve your presence; it is a privilege and not a right. Protect your energy at all costs, life will come with enough stress without dealing with people that set out with the intent to be condescending do to envy and jealousy. Wish them well but, do it from afar hopefully growth finds them and puts them in a better place.

7. **Today's Thought...Not getting what you want, when you are not prepared for it, can be the biggest blessing there is. There could be no greater disaster than wishing for something great and have it leave you behind do to you not being prepared ...#everythingsbetterinitstime#**

- Timing in life is one of the most important things to consider when it comes to the success of anything. A career, product or invention will all be affected by the "When". If something is created in a time where there is

- not a need the idea can and most likely will not be successful. If an opportunity comes and you are not yet prepared though it may be the one thing that you've always wanted the outcome would be tragic. Imagine seeing your dream pass you by. So, success and timing go hand and hand and when it lines up it can be a wonderful thing.

8. Today's Thought... "To learn more you simply need to talk less" I was watching a video the other day and a rapper by the name of Kevin gates said, "The reason you have two ears, and one mouth is so that you can listen twice as much as you speak." That was a very profound, it's hard to speak and hear at the same time. That's why silence is golden. #listen #learning #greatness #growthmindset #growth #hardworkpaysoffs

- Here is a very simple question, "If you were watching something that you need to learn would you talk the entire time or be quiet to actually hear the content?" Therefore, most people repeat mistakes simply due to not listening. If you are quiet, you can see if someone is being honest or not in business, and in relationships you can get clarity during a discussion if it is your desire to hear the person in an effort to rectify the situation. Learning is something everyone should strive to do every day and how better to do this then to be quiet during a teach-able moment.

9. Today's Thought...Being a father is one of the greatest things that you can be. If you don't believe me look at the state of the world and our children. We need more good ones...#weshapethelifesandbehaviorsofthechildren#

- Fatherhood is one of the most underappreciated roles in society today and the truth is it's probably the second most important role period. In the wild when a father is not present the children run wild due to the lack of a male presence keeping the children in line. Well, the same is true in society and you see this by the number of children that are involved in violent crime and the uptick in underage childbirth. The masculine presence in a daughter's life is what allows the feminine behavior to flourish. Only when a female feels protected is she able to be feminine and this security is provided by the male presence. The father is just as important as the mother in the life cycle of the child.

10. **Today's Thought... Ask yourself when was the last time that you had a good laugh, and if it's been a while try and find a way to get one. You'll be glad you did...**<u>#Laughteristhebestmedicineanditsfree#</u>

- There is an old saying that laughter is the best medicine, and it is literally the truth. When you laugh there are endorphins that are released that lowers blood pressure and reduces stress. Everyone could use these benefits during the ups and downs that we have experienced due to the pandemic that we are now in. With the amount of life lost during this time anxiety is at an all-time high. And the separation that you have had to experience from your family it's enough to weigh on anyone but, there is a way to alleviate the weight. How you say? Try every day to watch something that will make you smile you'll be glad you did and everyone around you will benefit too.

11. Today's Thought…"If you cannot be Hurt, you cannot Be Loved."

- Being emotionally vulnerable brings about one of life's greatest conundrums. We all want to love but, to do this you must be willing to take the chance of getting your heart broken. A guarded heart is theoretically not a bad idea I mean who wants to experience the hurt that a painful breakup can bring. But, to never love in the way that relationships are meant be is the biggest tragedy one could ever face. Is losing love painful? Of course, but to never has experienced love in its truest form is life's true tragedy.

12. Today's Thought...Being there for a friend doesn't cost a thing, but in that time of need to that friend in need, it's worth is priceless... #spreadlove#

- Some relationships are irreplaceable just as some friendships are closer than family ties, over time they become family. The ties that you build over time will make your bonds with friends closer than the ones that you have with some family members. Some people have friends that you have known as long as your actual family and by the time that you are an adult you will have spent as much time with the people as you have your own kin. So, remember this blood makes you related and bonds make you family.

13. Today's Thought...If you really want to know who your real friends are watch how they act after something good happens to you. It will bring out their true character ....#andeventhatisablessing#

- Sometimes favor will bring about jealousy and the hardest thing to have to digest is where the jealousy will come from. The reality is people are okay with you doing well just not better than them. And you never expect to see this from close friends, yet that's where it comes most often, and you never see it until something happens that elevates you from the crowd that you are in. This as strange as it may seem is still a blessing, you need to know who is in your corner truly. And life has a funny way of weeding out who should and should not be around you in times of triumph and tribulations. It may not feel good at the time but know that it's for your good.

14. Today's Thought...The greatest tragedy would be to get the one thing that you've wanted and not be prepared to receive and have it pass you by....#tragic#

- What if you had the opportunity to become the lead of a movie and it was a once in a lifetime break but, when it was time to get the part, you were told that you weren't good enough yet? Who is to say that the chance will ever come around again? And just to know that the only reason that you did not get the part due to preparation or lack thereof on your part. Regret would set into the point that you would get physically sick. So, to keep this from happening in every situation work hard, over pre-pare. In the words of a great man, "if you stay ready you don't have to get ready".

15. Today's Thought...No matter your age, Never stop dreaming!!! .. #realtalk#

- Having something to look to forward each day is one of life's motivating stimuluses. And dreams are just that, a source of power to be drawn from and in some cases, dreams are the motivation that one needs to continue to live. Dreams grow you due to being the subliminal possibilities of your existence. And you never know where theses desires to become will take you. In the movie Black Panther there is an actor that has tried to break into Hollywood for years and at age 81 she got her chance as one of the elders in the tribe. This is a perfect example that it's never too late to pursue your passion.

Prayer is...

16. Today's Thought...Once you've done all that you can, step back and let God work ... He'll Fix it .... #Godcannotfail#

-   Spirituality in life has been for me a source of hope that has been reinforced by action. And in some cases, after you've done all the work, some things just will not work out. This is when you must let go and let God have the wheel. The problem is we wait to the last minute to involve him. If I can say nothing else, I can say that he can and will fix most situations if we just get out of his way. Remember this, a lot of the time we are the problem.

17. Today's thought ... I just watched my little girl get on the bus and go to school and realized there is no going back to what she used to be. Where did the time go? Got to admit it hurt to see her go... ☹

- One thing is guaranteed in life over all else is change. Nothing will stay the same. Just as your children will become adults in what seems to be a blink of the eye. We go from young to old in a flash. I was talking to a friend about something that happened in High School and once we looked deeper into it, we were discussing something that happened over 30 years ago. The scary thing is it seemed like it just happened yesterday. Make the most of your time here because just like that it will be gone.

18. Today's Thought… "Build others Up" In a world that seems motivated to tear people and things down. Choose to be the one that builds people up. Suicide rates are higher than they have ever been and just think if you or someone else took the time to say the encouraging thing that would have given that person enough strength to make it another day. Everything is better with love. #goodvibes #spreadloveandkindness #lovewins #bekind

- The world can be a terrible place but, it can also be a very wonderful and beautiful place full of nature and wonder. Perspective is everything and your outlook is key to what your mindset is on life. Live every day to make someone's life a little easier and their day brighter. You never know what someone is going through and the interaction that you have could be the one thing that someone needed to keep them from taking their own life. If something looks off with someone that you interact with, please check on them this pandemic has people feeling alone and helpless. Kindness is free and it costs nothing to give to anyone so give it to everyone. Spread love every chance you get.

19. Today's Thought... My daughter makes me laugh, and she got it honestly, so my yesterday my 5-year-old and I were watching tv and she passes gas and she turned to me and said with hands raised," It happens sometimes daddy, it happens sometimes" slmbo!!!!

- Your children are a direct reflection of you, good or bad, and this at times can really make you laugh to see just who you are. It can also be very humbling to know the capacity for mistakes reflected in their actions. Being a good example is probably one of the most important jobs you have a parent, whether biologically or by adoption so when you see good things reflected it's you. But remember they see everything, even what you think they don't, and they live what they see.

20. Today's Thought…Do the work, greatness lies in two things, 1# when preparation meets opportunity and 2#all the things that you were willing to do that the next person wouldn't before the opportunity presented itself. Do the work #greatness #workinprogress #workharder #dontcomplain

- I once watched an interview of Kobe Bryant, and he talks about how he prepared for greatness. He would get up every day at 4 am and go to gym for 2 hrs. come home and then he'd go again at 8 for 2 hrs. and then again at 2pm for another couple of hours. He said by consistently doing this by the time he had repeated this grueling schedule the amount of basketball that played would separate him from his competition at a rate that they would never be able to catch up to him. It's always about the work, and if you work hard, you will be successful, but you must put in the sweat equity. So how bad do you really want to be great.

21. Today's Thought... Control is an illusion and logic are only as solid as the common sense that it is connected to ....

- Situations in life are as unpredictable as the weather, yet some will continue to stress themselves trying to control that which they cannot. Prepare yes, but just trust in your ability from preparation to handle whatever may come your way. And in the situation relax and think soundly because though you may not have the ability to control when events occur. You can have a direct effect on the outcome of what happens. Focus only on what you can control the rest will take care of itself.

22. Today's Thought…" I was told that it was noticed that I don't curse, and then asked Why? Which is more unbelievable the question or the questioned action?

- I never thought that I'd see the day in which class and decorum would be considered as overt. And the overt now the norm, class is still expected and if no one expects it from you then expect it from yourself. Shame is still a thing as well as accountability, and there may only be the few but if you stay solid the few will become the many. Remember it's not that you are better it just that you know better and choose to do better.

23. Today's Thought...Always make room for love. When you do that things now have the possibility of getting better.
#Positivethinkingequalspositivebeing

- There are some people who have turned their back on love. And I get it in a world that seems to be so cold and uncaring there are many reasons to protect your heart and keep people from getting in. But what is life with nothing to look forward to? What would be the point of our existence if not to look out for each other? Being kind and nice is one of the few things on earth that you can do for free. So, who will you bring kindness to today? It's the one thing that you give away that makes you feel better the more that you do it. Spread Love.

24. Today's Thought... A Great Dad is like a Brownie. Tough on the outside but soft in the inside.

-   Dads can come off grumpy and tough sometimes and I know I am guilty of this. But don't let this fool you at 6 foot 1 and 235 lbs. can I look intimidating? Yes, I can. And can I be intimidating, oh yes for sure. But let my kids need something or ask for something and all that goes the window. I become a big ole Teddy bear and they get whatever they want. With strength you must be able to know when to be soft, balance is necessary in this security is built. As much as you may want to be respected, and respect is necessary, but you must let you children as well as your significant other feel secure enough to bring what troubles them to you. Be more than a just a protector and disciplinarian be willing to listen.

25. **Today's Thought... Work on your issues, if not you will become your issue. Nothing worse that standing in your own way. I refuse to do it; I have haters for that ......**

- There is nothing worse than to hear a person say, "This is just the way that I am". What the other person hears when this is said is, that you don't want to do any better and everyone should be okay with it. All have had things in life happen to them and those things may or may have not been your fault. But even the things that were not your fault that have hurt you that caused whatever defense mechanisms that you have adapted are still up to you to fix. Your behavior is your behavior, and you control your mood as well as your response. Some peoples issues will keep them from maintaining a job and ultimately being successful. And if you need help, then there is nothing wrong with seeing a counselor. And even that is you doing something to improve. Mental health is one of the most important aspects of every person's life so please go and seek help if necessary. Don't be the reason that you can't get to become the best version of you.

26. Today's Thought...Do people really want honesty? Or do they want the answer that will make them feel the way that they want to feel.

#Truthorsecuritywhatwilluchoose#

- In relationships either intimate or interpersonal people will talk about things that are on their heart and at times you will find yourself trying to help them find a solution to what troubles them. What you must do is find out what are they really looking for? Do they just want to vent or, are they looking for a solution? The answer to that question will be just as different as the person that you are dealing with at the time. When we care we tend to look to see if we can find out how to solve the puzzle of their mind when sometimes they do not want the truth or even logic. They just want to be heard and to alleviate any stress and confusion before you speak on the matter find out exactly what they are looking for. You both will be glad that you did.

27. Today's thought... In the observance of thanksgiving, in the mist of the turkey and all the fixings, what are you truly thankful for???

- Thanksgiving is my favorite holiday, and it has always been that way from childhood. The smells, the smiling face of my mother as she would hand me the mixer and let me lick the cake batter off the blades. Spending time together with family is one of the most important things in life. And before you know it the memories are sometimes all you will have, and you will be thankful for the little things that you experienced together. I'm glad to have understood this early and to have taken the time to make memories with my loved ones while they were here. So, what are you thankful for?

28. Today's Thought...Great rewards never come without sacrifice....

<u>#towhommuchisrequiredmuchisgiven</u>#

- No saying has ever been truer than, "Great achievement is usually born of sacrifice". Or No pain no gain, these all lend themselves to the understanding that greatness and effort go hand and hand. People want all the flash with no substance. The microwave path to success without sweat equity if you do achieve it, you will not know how to maintain it. The hardest thing to do is to be disciplined, though it sounds simple most will struggle with it. Yet that ability is everything that will lead you to where you want to be in life.

29. Today's Thought...Be adventurous, only fear the unknown if it has teeth... #IJS#

- Sometimes it's just that simple be willing to try new things like foods, and travel destinations. In my travels I learned more and more about myself as I learned about the world. The Cultures the customs what a wonderful world are we on and how many wonders are there for you to experience if you just go. Now as beautiful as this world is, is as deadly as it can also be. So, enjoy yourself just always watch out for teeth.

30. Today's Thought...Change is necessary... <u>#realtalk</u>#

- Sam Cook authored a song many years ago entitled Change gone Come and he could not be more correct with that title. Change will happen whether you want it or not, even as you are reading this you will never again be the age you are now. Nor will you ever again experience this day again. So, the question becomes how will you contribute to your change? Will you take the reins and make your growth a great and wonderful thing? Or will you let time pass and you fade away into the dark without ever making your mark?

31. Today's thought...Whenever there is a period of organized hate, Genocide will soon follow. #Facts

- As history has shown us, Germany, China, Africa, and America all have shown the world this ugly truth. We are all part of the human race yet; it seems that the only thing that we in a rush to do is focus on what makes us different. When we should be highlighting the qualities that makes us the same. It will always be harder to hurt anyone that reminds you of yourself.

32. Today's Thought...there's no substitute for common sense......

- Common sense a term that seems so simple and yet complicated and so rare in practice. The word common sense per Webster's dictionary is "Sound and prudent judgement based on a simple perception of the situation or facts". Simply put it's a practice that should be understood by everyone. So, if that is the case why are things so divisive in our day-to-day living? Common sense should be the glue that makes life harmonious and allow people to come together. Let's get back to practicing those principals again could you imagine how things would be if we did?

33. Today's Thought ... What is your purpose??? Do you have an idea and are you fulfilling it? Live every day to be better that you were the day before ....

- There are some that will live their whole life and never find out what the purpose for their existence. I believe that most people that feel unfulfilled are in this condition. Here are some questions to ask yourself to put yourself on track to finding how to realize your purpose. 1) What can you do that you enjoy that you could do all day and never get tired of? 2) What are you great at that comes with the greatest of ease? Whatever that is find out the occupations that includes those skills and you will find yourself actually living and not just existing.

34. Today's Thought...Limitations are the ceilings that you set on you own potential...How high are your ceilings? Or do you have any?

- There is a saying that I've heard that says, "The person that believes they can and the person that believes that they cannot are both right". That tells you how powerful the mind is. What you can become no matter how great must first be visualized and then put into action. So, if you believe that there are limits to what you can achieve then you will only reach as high as the ceiling that you set for yourself. How high are you willing to let yourself go?

35. Today's Thought... Take out time to notice the little things, the big ones won't be jealous...

- In the middle of my busy week, I did something that don't usually do, I took some time and went bowling. Now that may seem like something small, but I swear it was the most fun that I have had in a while. I know that I love to bowl and doing it made me remember just how much. When life is moving at such a fast pace just remember every now and then to take care of you. You matter and as much as you may not realize it you deserve to be happy too. This one was personal to me so Ladies if you are reading this look out for your man, more than every now and then. And if you are a Man reading this book do something to make yourself smile. Let's get to this new normal, happy spouse happy house.

36. Today's Thought..." Why is truth so taboo now days?"

- People live every day to find out what their purpose is and while doing that indirectly they are seeking truth. The truth that they are looking for may be their own, yet it is still the truth. But in society we seem focused on doing all but admitting the truths in this world. The truth of science and the natural law, the truth of biology and the truth as it has always existed. Certain things cannot be disputed like gravity and the need for clean air. However now there is a debate on what a man is or what a woman is, and I never thought that we would be here. Be whatever you want to be in your life just don't try to force your way of thinking on me and I'll do the same.

37. **Today's Thought... Supporting others should be done without any expectations. Until you learn this rule don't expect anyone to support you in your ventures..#unconditionallove#**

- Having someone's back is a position in life that we all should practice. When you see someone attempting to become something positive support the effort. And expect nothing in return that is how spreading love works and the funny thing is when you do it will come back to you. Don't do it for show, do it because you genuinely want to see another human beings' attempt to be more than what they currently see themselves as become realized. All greatness started with two things and idea and someone's belief in the idea being made real. Until you can do this don't expect the positive energy returned in your life.

38. Today's Thought... Before you receive your blessings the road is always the hardest stay steadfast and just know that it's coming... #thestormwillclear#

- When pursuing a goal there will come a time when you ask yourself can I do this? At this crossroad is the path to two places, greatness, and regret. And only you will be the deciding entity that will determine the destination that you will arrive at. What will make the decision clear is the desire for your goal. Will you choose what you desire most or what you desire right now. Success is not for the faint of heart, but the rewards are worth the struggle that you endure. It's coming just keep working!

**39. Today's Thought... What have you done for your relation-
ship lately?**

- One of the most selfless questions that you can ask is
  what have you done for your relationship lately? But to
  do this you would have to put the other person in your
  relationship first. It sounds easy but, a lot of time people
  get so caught up in their life and their needs and wants
  that they forget about the other party. A relationship
  just like an automobile must have constant maintenance
  because little by little it will break down if it's not taken
  care of. A good practice is every now and then ask the
  other party if there is anything that you can do better or
  where you can improve. It's takes effort on both parts so
  just make sure you are doing your part. And if you have
  a good person, they will reciprocate the effort.

40. Today's Thought... Do something special for someone today..#thatisall#

- Try to spread Love every day and it doesn't have to be anything big, open a door for someone. Give a complement, help an elderly person with their things. Little things mean a lot and when you do with understanding that no one owes you anything it can make someone feel special. You have no idea what someone is going through in their daily struggles and that one glimpse of kindness could be the one thing that will give them hope that they wouldn't have otherwise had. And who knows if that is one gesture that kept them from taking their own life. #Spread love

41. Today's Thought..." Got Goals?" What is life without your next thing to look forward to?

- There is a belief that I have that you should always be trying to grow. Learn something daily or at least have the desire to. Nature shows us that anything that is not growing is dying and this pandemic has shown me that nothing stays the same, you are either doing one or the other. So, if you think that you are doing nothing, I assure you that you are probably declining. The sad thing is not a lot of people are taking this into consideration. No truer statement than complacency kills. So, what are you going to do to change it?

42. Today's Thought...Family is all you have...#ijs#

- No one loves you like family and if you have spent time with your family during holidays you understand the concept. How each of you look at each other, the laughter while the children play, and the sheer enjoyment of time spent together. Now there are other family members that are not blood. I have friends that I have known for over 30 years and though we may not share an ounce of DNA between us I would consider them family. I recently had a conversation with a friend, and we talked about being family and being related and how one is due to DNA and the other is due to relationship. Both are important and a necessary part of the human experience so make sure you take out the time to enjoy both.

43. Today's Thought..." The world needs to be refocused on what's really important."

- Every day on the news it seems that there's gun violence and discussions where there are two opposing parties disagreeing about something. And whether its gun rights, religion, race, or the haves verses the have nots. In everyone one of the disagreements the groups all have one thing in common. The focus is not on the reality that there is more that makes us similar than divides us. So why do we focus on the one thing that we don't agree on instead of the things that makes us similar? If we saw ourselves in the opposing views, we would work harder to fix it, than to win the agreement. In all those disagreements the one thing I see is wanting things to be better. Let's start there then, if we all work provide solutions instead of turmoil, we could fix it.

44. Today's Thought...Handle situations carefully, the outcome directly effects your quality of life. So however good or bad you live is controlled by your choices...#Choosewisely#

- Have you ever been in a situation and later thought I wish I had handled that differently? I believe we all have at some point and the only difference would be the degree to which the decision made effected your outcome. Some decisions can be made with little to no real effect to your existence. And some decisions can cost you your entire life. And all it takes is one wrong decision, some things you only get one chance to get it wrong and you can literally lose everything. So slow down and choose wisely for, your very life could depend on it.

45. Today's Thought… " Choose love, for when you do nothing else matters."

-   How you perceive a thing dictates how you treat a thing. So, if you choose to love It will cause you to want the best for whatever it is that you love. At times as people we forget that we are all having the same experience just in different ways simultaneously. And if we took that into account, we would probably have more empathy for everyone that we encounter every day. The world is one tribe, it's called "the human race" and if we focused on the similarities instead of what makes us different the existence that we would create would be harmonious in ways that we have never seen. So always choose love.

46. Today's Thought...Do all that you can so you can have no regrets... #learninghardlessons#

- This one for me is very personal and I would even go as far as say this was a trial through fire that caused me to learn this truth. We have a finite number of days on this planet and what you do with them matter. And in loss I have learned the value of this truth. The loss of my mother has taught me a lot, about myself and about the importance of the use of time and the value seizing the moment. I was able to say that I did whatever I could for her during her transition and it has given me a sense of peace. However, I still wonder even in this truth could I have done more? There has never been a truer statement than work while its day for night is coming. And what you do with your time is so very important because there is no coming back and it will become your legacy. The things that you accomplish are just as important as the things that you did not. Now let that sink in. Please don't leave unfinished business for once left that is the state in which your legacy will remain.

47. Today's Thought…God's greatness is usually shown when you are at your weakest …
<u>#sotherecanbenoquestion</u>#

- "When we are weak, he is strong" for those that aren't believers this may go over your head but, for those that are, once you have been on your sick bed you understand the gravity of this principal. Life has a way of showing you just how little power you have in situations, and it will put you in circumstances where you must lean on a higher power. No matter who you pray to this rings true. And the truth is I have even heard of instances where there were atheists who when in a volatile situation called out lord help me. Instinct tells you that there must be something greater than us to have allowed this whole existence to take place and to pay respect to it only makes sense. Just as it also makes sense to call for help when the circumstance is too much for you to endure to have the in your time of need. He/she will be there no matter who your "He/She" may be.

48. **Today's Thought... Be aware that whatever you are doing good or bad , someone is watching...**
#Dorightorkeepyaheadonaswivel#

- Someone always sees what you are doing. I don't care how good you think that you are hiding it at some point you will be found out. And it's not always a criminal matter that I'm speaking about. Morality is still a thing, and the bill always comes due. I don't care that the world says you can do what you want. There will be a day of reckoning and it will cost you in some way. So, when you go to make that decision and you hear that little voice that says don't do that, hopefully you listen because you may get away with it now but believe me it always comes out in the end. Some bells cannot be un rung so you better be able to live with the results.

49. Today's Thought...Have you planned this week to be suc-cessful... #youplaythewayupractice#

- Do you ever feel like you are working towards a thing but not making traction. If so, you need to check the plan, now if you are saying what plan, then we have another issue altogether. I have started doing something that has helped me become very productive and that is on Sunday I plan out everything that I plan to do during the week. Day by day I have goals and by planning that way, I have started getting so much done with much less effort. Little things like this will be the reason you achieve your goals and stay on Track.

50. Today's Thought...Get grounded, get focused... Now Forward!!!.. #letsgo#

- Sometimes life will have you feeling all over the place and this will have an adverse effect on your motivation. Too much inspiration can be just as troublesome not having enough. Sometime the having a lot of ideals that you never finish has the same result as doing nothing. Write is down or record the ideas and then prioritize them so that you don't lose the inspiration and have a way to finish the task at hand. One thing at a time, start and then finish the task moving is not the same as progress and some people don't know the difference between the two. One is just doing things and the other brings about results.

Read the fine print

51. **Today's Thought...Make sure you are sure and read everything for the small print will be your undoing. It's all in the details!** #Coveryouself#

- Have you ever heard the saying that the devil is in the details? What they are talking about is the small print. Court cases are either won or lost by your understanding of the small print. Lawyers make their living on the mastery of this truth. Take your time making decisions on big ticket items read the print carefully and make sure that you know the contact just as good as the company selling you the item or the service that you are trying to purchase. At some point this advice will save you a pretty penny and keep you from a lot of headaches. Or it will be the reason that you have a unfortunate experience at your own expense. **#Takeyourtime**

52. Today's Thought…" How beautiful you are!!!! Now keep repeating this until you believe it. "

-   The saying "Beauty is in the eye of the Beholder" is very valid statement but, what if the beauty that you are supposed to see is interpersonal? This is a little trickier especially if the one that needs to see it cannot. Seeing what you bring to table and your uniqueness is so important in a time when everyone is trying to be a copy of what they are seeing on TV or social media. To find the beauty in yourself you must first find out who you are. Who are you? Do you even know? Do you know why you exist? Start there once you do that the rest come into focus and the beauty that you bring will surprise even you.

53. Today's Thought...Sometimes breath mints are very essential ...#IJS#

- Sometimes you must ask yourself, is it me? People sometimes become oblivious to their own ability to be wrong. One of the best ways to remain humble is to never just assume that you are right. Just because you feel strongly about a situation doesn't equal being correct. Sometimes those strong biases can be the thing that clouds your ability to make a fair judgment on a situation. So, the next time someone offers you a breath mint, don't be offended just take one because it might be you.

54. Today's Thought...True strength is standing firm when something is right even if it is not the popular thing to do...#stillstand#

- The definition of strength can mean different things to different people. To some strength is the measure of the ability one to lift heavy things and how much of that ability that one possesses. And while having physical strength is a good thing this is not the strength that I'm speaking about. The type of strength that I am speaking about is moral strength. Morality is something that seems to be in short supply recently and if it doesn't worry you, it should. Social norms have been under attack just as the definition of truth. What is true is still true and what is right is still right. Stand firm on this truth there is something inside every one of us that tells us what is right and what is right. Listen to that voice, listen to the feeling that you feel when you know something is wrong don't give into these new norms do right and be strong. Live every day for a clear conscience and most of all always spread love.

SOMETIMES THERE ARE NO SECOND CHANCES, NO TIME OUTS, NO NEXT TIME. SOMETIMES IT'S NOW OR NEVER!

55. Today's Thought...Seize the moment in some things you don't get a second chance ... #truth#

- There is a statement that I read recently, "Pain is Temporary, Regret is forever". The truth in that statement is almost haunting to one's life review. Always shoot your shot if you have an opportunity. Go for it even if you fail. I believe that you learn more from your failures than you do your successes. When you are trying to find your way in life knowing what you are not good at is probably more important than knowing what you can do. With knowing one it makes your decisions more concise because you eliminate clutter and can focus on the positive movement. With that each decision you make, your path becomes clearer and you destination closer with each step you take. So, keep the what if's away or at least minimal so you can become the best version of yourself that you can possibly be.

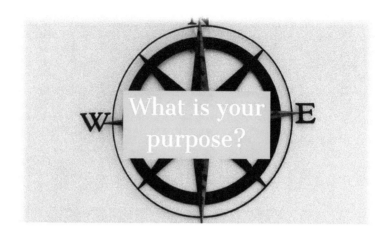

56. Today's Thought...Unfulfilled is the one that knows everything except how to be themself ...

#youcantbecompleteuntillyouknowyourpuropse#

- This one is for the person who is being crushed under the weight of other's expectations. Although they may mean well there is only one you. No one can tell you how to be you so, every attempt that one takes in advising someone should be to help you find you how to be your best version of yourself. Unfortunately, people get lost in that part of the journey. You must live your life and become whatever you are passionate about. But just know even this comes with a reward and good or bad, if you can live with what it includes, then do so. Purpose equals peace remember that. Live well.

57. Today's Thought...Every step that you make in life, SHOULD be carefully thought about. For once a decision is made there is no going back... #realtalk#

- Have you ever heard the statement "Measure twice cut once" well if not it's a statement that originated in the carpenter's profession. It shows the importance of taking time and making the right decision. You can't uncut wood so when you finally cut the piece you must live with the result of your decision. In the case of wood, when a mistake is made you can just get another piece but, when it comes to a life decision some decisions can only be made once. If the decision is wrong at the wrong time, someone can lose their life. Though the example may be an extreme the principal is valid none the less. So be very careful, take your time and don't make rash decisions.

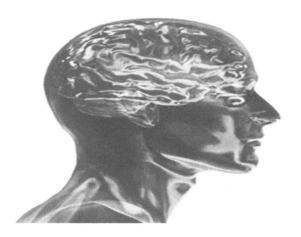

58. **Today's Thought…You are what you eat, have you ever heard of a person getting fat off Vegetables? You know what, Me neither, have you ever seen someone be successful and be full of negative thoughts, nope. Ingesting negative things be it food or thought affects the whole being. So, what are you allowing in your temple?** #protectyourpeace #BuildYourTemple

- There is no truer principal than, "You are what you eat". The eating is not the part that causes the issue it's the ingestion of what's consumed that is the true culprit. Ingestion in its simplest form is what's absorbed. And food isn't the only thing can be ingested, how about images or ideals that you wouldn't deem healthy like Pornography or programs that include violence or the use of drugs. You must protect your mind like you protect your body for as the mind goes so does the body. **#Spreadlove**

59. Today's Thought…"Give the day it's mood" When you wake up, say three things for which you are thankful. And then after that tell the day that it's going to be good," this is going to be a good day". The energy will obey leading you to a new understanding of positive thinking. You are going to have a good day!!!! #protectyourpeace #positivevibes #mindsetmatters

- When you get up in the morning set the tone for the day. How do you do that you ask? Well first say everything that you are thankful for. You will be surprised how something so simple can be so instrumental in setting not just the day's mood but your mood as well. When I go into a place, I say what I want to happen when I am there, and I would have to say more than not it seems to happen just the way I wanted it to. Speak life and life will happen, for there is the power of life and death in the tongue. #Speaklifeandspreadlove

60. Today's Thought…" Are your feelings your own? Or you a good impersonation of what everyone wants you to be? "

- How do you feel about the state of your affairs? Do you like who you are and more importantly if you don't, are those your views or views of others persuading your opinion of yourself? Societal pressures and social norms are used to keep morality in check and that can be both good and bad. Overt behavior should be kept in check however, there is a difference between the overt and an opinion of life choices. Sometimes friends, family and parents will inadvertently put pressure on you to become something that may not be in your life's destiny with the best intentions in mind. Being a lawyer, Doctor, are great things however, your passion will always bring you to the truest version of you and that will help you find your purpose. That is the end game, finding your reason for existing and once you do peace will come. Do what you love, and it will lead to you loving you.

61. **Today's Thought...You are the master of your own mind, you control its thoughts, You control how you let your thoughts make you feel... But if you can't please get help it's the best thing you can do for yourself...#Thinkaccordingly#**

- The hardest thing you will ever do is gain mastery of your mind, if you don't believe this look at the amounts of mental illness and anxiety cases worldwide and then compare them to the levels even 20 years ago. During the pandemic mental illness and anxiety numbers have exploded. It's understandable with all the uncertainty to be unsure during this time with record loss of life. And getting help is a good thing everyone needs help in life please don't hesitate to get the help you need. You are important and loved, there is only one you. No one else can play your part so take care of your mental health. #Everyoneneedshelpsometimes

Positive Energy
(Aust)

62. Today's Thought...There is a scientific principal that states, "energy is neither created or destroyed but changed from one form to another." What if all the energy that is used to do wrong was changed in effort to help somebody? What a place the world would be...#Utopia#

-    Have you ever been in the presence of someone and for whatever reason you got a bad feeling, and you didn't understand why? Or have you ever been around someone, and you felt a comforting feeling and you didn't know them well? For both cases what was happening was you were able to read their energy. Energy by nature has both positive and negative charges and it takes on a nature simply due to the intentions of the user of the energy. So, what if everyone chose to love what a wonderful world would it be, so remember your intentions are what shapes the world.

63. **Today's Thought... Life is not fair sometimes however the reward makes all the pain we endure worth it in the end. To learn patience is to obtain peace in its most basic principle.**

- I was once told that everything in life is either one of two things, it's either a lesson or a blessing. The truth is in a lot of instances life is not fair but, it is worth living even in the bad times. The amount of beauty that life holds alone makes it worth the experience. And sometime the most painful of life lessons are the most important principals that you had to learn. And the lessons that you will never forget. Remember that life and death are both equally important to existence.

64. Today's Thought...Strive for perfection in an imperfect world, you owe it to yourself...#asuwere#

- The best thing you can do for yourself, and others is become the best version of you that you can. It does two things #1) If you are constantly growing it keeps depression and anxiety from affecting you. And #2) Your growth will inspire others in ways you will not understand. Working to become who you are meant to be will keep regret at a minimum and personal satisfaction at a maximum. But most of all it will allow you to be able to help others more proficiently due to your acquired resources and knowledge. Keep growing and spreading love, you owe it to everyone.

65. Today's Thought...Success is achieved by doing, thinking about the goal will only get you so far...#readytogrind#

- A well thought out plan is a great thing if implemented correctly it will allow you to be efficient and successful in most endeavors. But the most important part of success is the doing. For anything to be accomplished you must act, all else is just talk. Anyone that was ever successful had to do one thing first and that thing was move. Taking that first step is the one thing that separates talkers from doers. And it's just that simple. Now Move!!!!!

66. Today's Thought…Faulty thinking is responsible for anything done that is deemed nonproductive or destructive by humanity… #thisworldneedsareboot#

- What is faulty thinking you ask? It is any thought or ideology that is conceived with the purpose of negatively affecting anyone or anything. There are entities that exist to destroy or interfere with the progress of productive actions in human relations. Be it environmental hazards or intentional attempts to keep groups of people from having necessary resources that they need. There are enough resources for everyone so, be willing to help your fellow human beings. We are all having a human experience, should we not have access to the same opportunities? If you see people being mistreated in this manner you must step up and stand with them. If not, at some point you will be the one needing to have someone stand up for you. Don't let your silence be the reason that someone is mistreated. **#Spreadlove**

**67. Today's Thought...Remove anyone or any-
thing that keeps you from seeing or thinking
clearly...#impairedthinking=complicatedlife#**

- One of the worst things that can happen to progress is having good intentions but getting bad advice.
  Sometimes the vision that you may have can be
  destroyed or delayed due to not having the correct
  plan in action. Moving and progress are two completely different things. Moving does require effort
  but, with that effort you tend to yield minimal results.
  Progress is effort that brings about a desired result.
  And being around the wrong people will only bring
  about moving without progress. So, keeping the right
  people around you are just as important as having the
  right plan in place. Not everyone should have access
  to you or your vision. Protect your energy and peace

there is nothing wrong with withholding your presence from those that don't appreciate or respect you. **#<u>Someplacesyouwillhavetotravelalone</u>**

68. **Today's Thought...Your visible actions are who most people want you to be or how you want to be perceived. Your secret thoughts are who you really are...**#thinkaccordingly#

- In most cases this is true, the person that you present in public is what I like to call your representative. It's the person that you are told that you are supposed to be. This person shows up at church, your job, and most public situations. Now the true person that you are shows up at home behind closed doors or when you are out with the boys or girls. And then there's you when no one is around that is the primal you. So, if you really think highly of your self do a true assessment of your thoughts when you are completely alone. I guarantee that it will humble you and let you know that there is still work to do on yourself. And that's good, just do the work. There's always room for growth. #Spreadlove

**69. Today's Thought....Living life while having expecta-
tions and setting goals will guarantee that you will
continue to grow and learn. Keep Growing my friends
...#Havesomethingtolivefor#**

- Goals should be set weekly; everyone should have a
plan each week that puts them further along on life's
path then the week before. Expectations should be
placed on yourself, the pressure that you put on yourself is a good thing. I would compare it to working out
in the gym. That push keeps you growing and gives you
something to strive for. I have seen with my own eyes
the results of having no expectations or goals i.e., purpose. I worked with some people and without naming
names once they retired, in under 6 months some of
these people literally passed away and I believe that it
was due to having no purpose. And if you are retired,
please keep learning or just helping for you have so
much to give.

70. Today's Thought...Focus is energy used from a properly placed obsession ... #Turninganegitiveintoapositive

- Obsession is a word that people usually look at in a negative light and people tend to not understand that even that form of energy if directed correctly can be very useful. The meaning of this would be focus. I have watched Kobe Bryant get into a Zhen like focus that is almost eerie. Most greatness takes a laser like focus that is almost seen as an obsession, and I would say that to be truly great you would have to be obsessed with the thing that you do. Now if his focus led to his work ethic in basketball just think if we worked with that level of intensity to help each other or to be kind to one another. I think focus when applied to something positive can only be good for everyone. And I try daily to better myself with focusing on improving the way I deal with my family. In what area will you work to focus on and improve? **#focusdanielson #karatekidfunny**

71. Today's Thought…"Why waste a profound sense of direction on finding destination nowhere?

- There are people that you will encounter that seem to have all the answers but, when you look at where they are in life, that's when the truth comes out. I call this the flash over substance syndrome. It's the wanting to look the part without doing the work. If those people worked as hard to gain the skill as they do to look like they, have it altogether. They would actually accomplish having it together. And regardless of what they say you still must do the work or at the end the truth will find you out. So, what you use your energy on is very important. For the destination is what makes the journey worthwhile. **#Flashorsubstance**

72. Today's Thought… Getting Organized can be one of the most useful tactics to help you accomplish anything, so why now use that effort to achieve something positive. #Facts

- Organizing for a cause can be helpful when the intentions are pure and helpful. However, when the same effort is used to render hate it can be catastrophic for the object being focused upon. And if the effort is not kept in check historically it becomes fatal for the group that is has been deemed the opposition. So please be careful with what you choose to lend you energy to. Remember this, the Kul Klux Klan thought that they were right too. **#Justbecuaseagroupofpeoplebelieveit dosentmakeitright**

73. Today's Thought...Live to be a blessing to someone else... #simple#

- This is something that I try to do every day, being kind is something that you can be to others that doesn't cost a thing. You would be surprised how far a smile in certain situations will go. Just doing that has led to many opportunities that granted me favor due to simply being hospitable. Being kind is its own reward, read that again. Although, it can make others feel better in the moment, life has a way of rewarding you because of your willingness to do for others. And I understand that most are giving to get but, I have seen how this principal works. Please, take out time to do something for someone else and expect nothing in return. It's just good to be good.

74. Today's Thought...Vision, Structure, and action= Success.

- Have you ever witnessed a house being built? The length of time that it may take the building from start to finish. To be completed, the process of planning starts months before the building ever begins. For the project to be successful there very carefully thought-out plans that must be put in place and steps followed before a nail hammered or piece of wood has been cut. So, everything must be done in its proper time. If you move too soon you will waste resources and, if the planning is not complete the build may not be successful at all. So first, a vison be presented then, the structure put in place, and after all this has been done the plan must be put into motion for anything to be accomplished. **#Seeplando**

75. Today's Thought...Time is no one's friend, work accordingly ...#iestopwastingit!!!

- The biggest enemy of mortality is time no matter the size of the person or the strength of the individual. Time always wins at some point you figure out that you will become less. In time you will become less capable than you once were yet, at the same time you become more. More intelligent and more responsible and the area that you increase your ability is in the legacy department. If you are lucky enough to make it to this point you will have less years in front of you than behind. When you do you will get an urge to do as much as you can to leave a legacy. One of the truest things I have ever heard is, "Work while its day for night cometh when no man can work". And the night that is spoken of is death. So, while you are here create all the greatness that you can, make all love you can. How you are remembered is your legacy. And when someone talks about you in the end make sure that you were one to be revered and

respected but most of all missed. For night is coming …
#Timeisthemostvaluablereasource

76. Today's Thought…" Got Goals?" What is life without the next thing to look forward to?

- There is a saying that life should be in a constant state of transition. For this to be true, one of two things are happening. You are either growing or dying, there is no in between and if you aren't pushing yourself forward then you know which of the two that you are doing. But the beauty of the situation is that you can choose which one that you become. And you can choose at any moment that you wish. And even better is knowing that all you must do is start will a little effort to change your status. You could be a little overweight due to the pandemic and you could simply decide to start walking outside. Or your job is not paying the bills the way that you need it too, simply look for another position or, go to school to retool yourself. Those were two basic versions of sparking growth in your life. So, what next on your life's agenda.

77. Today's Thought .... Ready or not here life comes, so stay ready and stay prayed up...#realtalk

- You ever just have one of those days? Or weeks? Recently I have heard story after story of tragedies, and it seems that they are coming without ceasing. Be it loss due to the pandemic, or just hardships that people are experiencing because of circumstances that come about. I don't know if you are spiritual or not but, for those that are stay prayed up. And for those that aren't look for the brighter side in the storm for even in the middle of the trial there are normally lessons that you can learn from. Or even moments of positivity that you can hold on to that will help you get through the situations that will come. So, stay ready so that you don't have to get ready. **#Lifewillcomebutyoucanmakeit**

78. Today's Thought...Not Everyone will love you, but you can still love Everyone!!! Spread Love!!!!!

-   Interpersonal relationships can be a wonderful thing. Most people will try to maintain pleasant report with one another. And it's one thing that makes life wonderful to experience. However, in times of disagreements amidst the tension it will make you not want to deal with anyone. But still love anyway even if you must love at distance do that. Just because you should love doesn't mean accept mistreatment either. You may have to remove yourself from a situation to protect yourself and most of all your peace. But don't stop loving just be smart and give your presence to those who deserve it. Not everyone deserves access to you. However, even then as hard as it may be, love anyways you don't know what someone may be facing. Hurt people, hurt people so, just love them where they are. **#Spreadlovealways**

79. Today's Thought... The easiest way to fail is to never try...

-   Any attempt to achieve something should be considered a win. Even if you are not good at a thing the knowledge gained from that experience is beneficial. For once gained the understanding can put you on the track to find out what you can be great at. But how could you get closer to finding out one's purpose if you never try. That is failure simply because you never gave yourself a chance to even know what you could become. That's why you must try at least once. If you are afraid, do it afraid but, do it just the same. Bravery doesn't mean not afraid it means you did the feat despite your fear. That is courage but if you never at least attempt then you've already lost. **#Alwaystry**

80. Today's Thought..." Choose love, for when you do nothing else matters."

- There is a theme in this book to always choose love and there is no truer statement than that. If you do that in most situations the outcome will be positive, simply due the intentions. Intentions are three forth of the crime and I have learned recently it makes more sense to focus on the intentions than the outcome. Sometimes you can have the best of intentions, but things do not materialize the way you wanted them to. But that is a rarity and when you choose to love most time the intentions are felt and understood and all it takes is a little communication and a cool head and reasonable conclusion can be achieved. So, intend to be loving and love will happen. **#Youarewhatyouintendtobe**

81. Today's Thought...In your life achievement wise, do you push yourself hard enough???

- I question myself in this manner often because I want to be the best version of me possible. What does that mean to you? For me it means that when I reach my final resting place that I have given the world and my family everything that I had and, I tried my hardest to give them everything that I could, my time included. Are there things that you want to learn and if so, would you really try to learn them? I mean really put in the work to master a new skill. I pride myself with trying to constantly improve. And for me it's more than just words. Even now I am writing my first book something that I always wanted to do, and I am almost finished with it. But what could you add to your skill set that you would work to do? Whatever it is keep growing always.

82. Today's Thought…"When you are going through something, and you feel that your overwhelmed stop for a second and just breathe your emotions will settle and clarity will come, feelings are temporary."

- As a musician I always have anxiety when I first go to learn a new piece of music so this was a lesson for me that allowed me to grow in that area. Situations will come that you just will not be prepared for and when they do come it is natural to have apprehensions about the unknown. So, when it comes, and you are feeling the pressure just stop and close your eyes and breathe and just wait. Don't move until you feel your feelings regulate and they will it may take a minute or two, but it will come, and you will be able to conquer the task at hand. **#Thistoowillpass**

83. Today's Thought...Experiencing life is its own reward...#spreadlove#

- Some of the best lessons that are learned are done simply by experiences and life's lessons are no different. Most of the growth that you do as a human being is done in your adult life and it's all done my experiences. Good and bad all the things that you go through are one of two things and that would be a lesson, or a blessing. Just by enduring if you live long enough you will learn so much by everything that you see. Because certain things books just don't explain in the way that doing the act will. So go, live, love but most of all grow and if all else fails spread love.

84. Today's Thought…Don't accept unreasonable situations , don't hope, make change happen…#fixtheproblem

-   Change is never easy especially when it comes to social norms. So, in most cases it takes very hard and necessary tactics to make the change that is needed. Hoping for change will only get you disappointed. Getting in the trenches is the only way to truly get change. Now when it comes to inner growth as a person it takes the same thing. Forming new healthy behaviors is one of the hardest changes to make and it doesn't happen overnight. But with consistency it does happen.

85. Today's Thought...What can be done today, should be done today ...#asuwere#

- Procrastination causes people that would ordinarily be successful into a life of mediocrity. A lack of discipline can be that catastrophic to one's upward trajectory. And it's completely unnecessary when all it takes is a little effort and planning to be able to be successful. A few intentional minutes and one can live a different tax bracket. So please don't put things off, you don't know how doing that will keep you from a life of achievement.

86. **Today's Thought...If you practice positivity, then you will be positive and your outlook dictates your mood...**#Tipsinbeinghappy#

- One of the most underused skills today is the use of positive thinking. If you have experienced a lot of trauma, it can be very hard to find the silver lining in things and that is understandable. Just start where you are with something simple like the beauty of the day and how nice the weather is. Just something simple can give you a few minutes of relief from your reality. And build there for even taking baby steps is still forward movement. **#Onwardandupward**

87. Today's Thought...Reinvention of one's self is necessary for growth...#shedtheoldyou#

- One of the most beautiful things that you will behold is the life cycle of a butterfly. Initially as a larva, it moves along the ground slowly and then one day magically it forms a cocoon and when it re appears the beauty that you see is undeniable. But before the beauty came the process and the truth is a lot of people want to skip the process, i.e., the work. From time to time, you will need to find out what's next for you. And that takes work, change is the one thing that should be constant in your life. Evolution is life's way of surviving so why would it be any different for the life path of any person. You must shed the old you to become thing new. Sometimes it's just as simple as trying something new to become what you've never been.

88. Today's Thought...A days' worth is given to it by the people you spend it with, not by the title of the day... #realtalk

- People get so caught up in titles or event names that at times they forget the importance of the people that they are sharing the experiences with. September 23, 2014, to most that is just a date in the past, no historical reference or importance to most lives. To me it was the day that time stood still. It's the day that my mom passed away. Now I'm not saying this to make anyone sad. However, I am saying this to do one thing, make you understand the importance of presence and to emphasize that time is finite and so is the time with people that you care about. So, take out time to spend with everyone that you hold dear and don't wait until an "Holiday" to do so. Because you may not get the chance. **#Spreadlove**

89. Today's Thought... Knowing when to keep quiet is just as important as knowing when to speak. And sometimes you must speak whether or not danger is a concern because the matter is bigger than your safety... #Sometimesyouhavetotakeonefortheteam

- In history people have lost their lives simply due to the words that they spoke at a certain moment. And the thing is they knew that if they spoke at that time, they would more than likely lose their life due to their stand on the issue. And the inverse is also true where there were people who wouldn't not have achieved greatness if they hadn't spoke up and have the guts to step into greatness. Each instance brought about a remarkable change in their lives. The first instance the person that lost their live was Martin Luther King and though he lost his life it was a speech he felt he had to make no matter the cost. Amelia Earhart was the other example, and no female prior ever flew solo around the world before her. Both made their marks and changed history. One spoke with action and other with words. Both made their mark in history.

90. Today's Thought...Are you accepting who you are? That is a critical question to ask of yourself as you navigate your life, your career, your relationships, and other areas of your life.

-   This question is important for a few reasons and one of the main reasons is sometimes you are not at peace with yourself. Due to not accepting who you are. The importance in the realization of who you are is that you can find yourself closer to your purpose when you know who you aren't. Or, if you are in a situation where you aren't happy have you just accepted it or, are you willing to do the work to change it. Regret is one of the worst things that you can have to live with and especially if you know that you can change it. Just know good or bad it always starts with you, and you do have the ability to fix it. So, what's your next move gonna be? #Itsgoingtogetbetterstill

91. Today's Thought… In most instances hate is just misplaced admiration, so even your haters have a purpose, so continue to inspire them. Let your actions speak.

- People cannot dislike something that they don't know exists. So, know that they're watching and while you are doing, they probably wish that it was them doing what they see you accomplishing. I have never understood the emotion of hate for I want everyone to win. And if you are interested in whatever that person is doing instead of being envious why not learn the skill and master it, that would be a better way to you use the energy of hating someone that choose to achieve. And if you are being hated on use the energy and work even harder. Don't you dare let up. They know that you are on your way let them watch you get there. **#Finishstrong**

92. Today's Thought...You must enjoy the journey just as much as you enjoy the destination. How you got there is just as important as where you are trying to go.

- This is something that I think really goes on that is not talked about enough. Everyone wants the microwave version of success, and no one wants to celebrate the process. The process is the most important part of the achievement. Just knowing that you are stronger today than you where yesterday due to the effort should be inspirational. And as you come closest to your goal your self-esteem and sense of pride is growing step by step. If more were able to fall in love with the process that would be the catalyst to keep you in state of growth always. And I've seen people get to the destination and get saddened with realization that it's now over. So, I would recommend that you always have goals. No matter what age, keep growing.

93. Today's Thought… Class and Shame has their place in society, that is how you keep overt behavior in check.

- Call me a dinosaur but I love people with standards, and I choose to live that way. I recently watched the Grammy Awards and when I saw the show there was a performance when two ladies were "performing" in such a way that I had to stop watching the "performance" due to the overt nature of dancing. Just because you can do something doesn't mean that you should. Freedom doesn't mean do whatever you want. There is still a penalty for actions and there will always be. The bill always come due, and it may not happen immediately and those are the hardest lessons to learn. And this generation is going to learn this principal. The sad thing about it is that when they learn it, it will be too late. So, if I can recommend class in your actions, please know that it still goes a long way. **#Ladiesandgentlemen**

Moments of DECISION

94. Today's Thought…In times of trouble before you decide on an action get still and wait. Once you are calm see if the decision you choose to make is the same as when the situation occurred. If so, you were probably on the right track all along.

- The lesson that was learned here was one that I think made the most difference in my life and if you can apply this you will make better decisions, and this will create better opportunities for you. The reason that this is necessary is because it gives you a chance to figure out a very important thing which is what the intentions behind the move was. The intention to me is now more important than what happened. Accidents happen but, if I know that no malice was intended then I will be quicker to forgive and move on. So, finding out the intent is more important the result.

Detox
FOR
RESTORING PURITY
Elements that assist with removing internal waste, toxins, and impurities.

95. Today's Thought...When did Ignorance become the accepted norm and common sense become the deviant culture?

- A while back I took a break from social media because I had to detox from seeing intentionally bad behavior. When did It become ok just to disrespect and think that there will be no consequences? In a lot of the videos people got hurt due to people not being ok with what they did. Here's reality when you do something you have no control over how someone else responds to the situation. But if you are doing something kind then more than likely you will receive kindness in return. Hopefully someone reads this and chooses to live in this manner. In the midst of the storm, try kindness it always works.

96. Today's Thought… Are you a good or great friend??

- In your lifetime you are lucky to have 3 great friends for your entire life. I mean real friends that you can talk to about anything. There are different types of friends You have the Party friend that is the one friend that is always down for a good time but not good a talking about topics of substance. Next you have the acquaintance, this is the type of friend that you hang with sometimes, you are cool but not to point that you trust them with all your truths. Then you have the REAL friend this person knows you inside and out those one's are made of gold and few and far between. So, what would you consider yourself? It's good to know that and depending on where you are in life just know there is always time to grow if you are willing to put in the work.

97. Today's Thought… Take advantage of life, and not the people in it…

- In life there are opportunities that will come your way due to relationship that you have nurtured. Take advantage of those opportunities to propel yourself and your family forward but never take those people that extended those opportunities for granted or use them. Good people are few and far between and your network is everything at the end. I have learned that success and your network is hand in hand. Always be moving towards the goal but not at the risk of your connections.

98. Today's Thought ...Insist on yourself. Never imitate...
<u>#Thatswhygodmadeoneyou</u>#

- There will be times that people will try to make you change to fit other narratives. Understand the difference between growth and selling out. Certain changes are good and necessary to be successful and to allow you to move in bigger rooms but, not at the risk of your principals. Never shrink yourself to make people comfortable and never accept disrespect to gain elevation for when you do just know that the energy you accepted to get you the position is the energy that will continue to receive when while you are there so set the precedence. You must teach people how to treat you.

GENDER WARS

99. Today's Thought ... I wish that there were no more of the battle of the sexes. The understanding is we need each other. It's time to make families cool again. #Thenaturalorderneedstoberestored

- I listen to the sentiments of both men and women in the modern era and to be honest it's quite sad. No one trusts each other which makes love almost impossible and in this era of social media the level of access to everyone that you've ever known is a form of sabotage all its own. There is a way back to love, but it takes for period of unlearning of these terrible habits and implementations of new norms. Boundaries need to be set but for that to happen people need to become trustworthy again. You must live intentional to be successful in love. It can be done.

100. Today's Thought...Always finish what you started …
<u>#lyfemadesimple</u>#

-   While raising kids there was a rule that I had and it was ironclad, if you start something (sports, instruments) you must finish it. There is no quitting. I believe how you practice is how you play so, for adults the practice time in life is your youth. And the habits that you start when you are young will continue into your adult life. And as I finish this book, I want to thank any who is reading this book for listening to my thoughts and points of view for living I hope that you enjoyed it and thanks for taking the time out read it. I finished it!!!!!! **#Ifinishedit**